THE MEANINGS OF MODERN ART

by JOHN RUSSELL

Art Critic, *The New York Times*

VOLUME 7

THE DOMINION OF THE DREAM

THE MUSEUM OF MODERN ART, NEW YORK

I. Giorgio de Chirico
The Anxious Journey, 1913
The Museum of Modern Art, New York

2

Dreams and dreaming are fundamental to human life; and in just about every work of art that is worth discussing a dream has somewhere been caught and completed. The impossible has been made to happen: we are face to face with what is, and yet is not; with what is not there, and yet is most vividly present to us.

This applies as much to the cooking pots and the half-peeled lemon in a still life by Chardin as it does to the stately forward march of Plato and Aristotle in Raphael's *School of Athens*. Such paintings perpetuate something that comes to the rest of us only momentarily, and when the dream makes poets of us all.

Since 1900 it has become clear to us that we dream because we need to dream. We do not dream at random, but in ways dictated by our own inmost nature. Rightly interpreted, the dream will reveal that inmost nature to us. The key event in this development was the publication in 1900 of Sigmund Freud's *The Interpretation of Dreams,* in which a central status was claimed for something that had until then been regarded as marginal to the serious business of life. "He is a dreamer. Let us leave him," says one character to another in Shakespeare's *Julius Caesar*; and the dreamer is by tradition someone of whom no effective action can be expected. But after 1900 people began to realize that the dream was the one department of life in which nobody fakes. In the dream, and there only, do we have direct access to the unconscious. "The dream," C. G. Jung wrote many years later, "is a little hidden door into the innermost and most secret recesses of the psyche." In the dream we lead a supplementary life: as Jorge Luis Borges puts it in his *Labyrinths,* "While we are asleep in this world, we are awake in another one; in this way, every man is two men."

In the novels and plays and poems by which our imagination is nourished, the dream operates for the most part as an early warning system. It brings an urgent, uncensored message from the unconscious. No matter how firmly we repress that message in our waking hours, it will steal upon us in our sleep. It is not always explicit. It is likely, in fact, to come upon us as an enigma. Sometimes we can un-riddle it, sometimes not. And a comparable strangeness characterizes some of the very greatest works of art. In Giorgione's *The Tempest,* in Rembrandt's *Polish Rider,* in *The Fortune Teller* by Georges de La Tour, life is stilled and suspended. Learned people can tell us that in the Giorgione an emblem of martial valor, on the left, is balanced by an emblem of womanly abandon on the right; that in the *Polish Rider* there is an echo of the skeleton horse and its skeleton rider which Rembrandt had seen in an anatomy theater in Leyden; and that the Georges de La Tour is not about fortune-telling at all, but about the gulling of a rich and inexperienced young traveler. But none of this will explain the particular spell of these pictures or the belief, common to all of us, that in looking at them we have access to a privileged state of mind. There is a literal explanation, but there is also something else: and that something else is the dream. At such times we are at one with Edgar Allan Poe, who once wrote that:

> All that we see or seem
> Is but a dream within a dream.

But Poe died in 1849; and from his position in time he could write those lines with an unself-consciousness which would be impossible today. He could not have foreseen to what extent the dream would be upgraded in our century. In Poe's day it was the prerogative of the artist to make sense of his dreams; the dreams of other people were thought of as either a suburb of Spooksville or a wishful incident in an otherwise pedestrian existence. Today people go to their dreams as in ancient Greece they went to Delphi: to consult the oracle. It was Jung's belief that "all consciousness separates": that from the first moment of self-awareness man begins to stand apart from other men, and from such elements in his own nature as he finds shameful or inconvenient. It is by censoring our selves that we build an acceptable social nature; "but in dreams," Jung went on, "we put on the likeness of that more universal, truer, more eternal man who dwells in the darkness of primordial night. Out of these all-uniting depths there arises the dream—infantile, grotesque, or immoral as it may be."

So radical a shift in human attitudes was bound to be reflected in painting. In such matters the arts sometimes race ahead of the sciences, much as a solitary horseman could once race ahead of a covered wagon. For an image of Jung's "all-uniting depths" nothing could be more telling than the vast rumination on the triad of E-flat major with which Wagner begins *The Ring*; yet Jung published that remark in 1934, while Wagner wrote in 1853. In literature there was gradually constituted throughout the 19th century an international confederation of the dream. Its founder-members included an Englishman, Thomas de Quincey; a German, E. T. A. Hoffmann; an American, Edgar Allan Poe; and a Frenchman, Charles Baudelaire. Another Englishman, Lewis Carroll, proved with *Alice's Adventures in Wonderland* (1865) that it was not only to a heavyweight adult literature that Jung's "little hidden door" would swing open. The dominion of the dream had been staked out in literature (and incidentally in art by Max Klinger [fig. 4], Odilon Redon, the Douanier Rousseau and others) long before Freud gave it clinical sanction.

1. Henry Fuseli
The Nightmare, 1781
The Detroit Institute of Arts

In one or another of its variants, Fuseli's *The Nightmare* became a classic of the late 18th-century imagination and an unforgettable image of night thoughts at their most unwelcome.

2. Paul Cézanne
The Murder, c. 1870
The Walker Art Gallery, Liverpool

Thirty years before Freud published his *Interpretation of Dreams,* Cézanne brought to this invented scene of violence an imagination as ferocious as it was concise.

3. Balthus
The Mountain, 1937
Private collection, New York

As late as 1937 the dream was still present as an animating force in ambitious art. Is the sleeping girl in the foreground of Balthus's painting simply asleep? Or is she dreaming the strange human scene around her, with its stylized attitudes, its talkers frozen in mid-sentence, its deliberately anachronistic look? Whether implicit or explicit, the dominion of the dream is absolute in this huge picture.

All this corresponded to deep-lying needs that were peculiar to their time. The French poet and dramatist Victor Hugo put that very well when he wrote of the 19th century as "the daughter of a religious past who sees in herself the mother of an industrial future." This dual, transitional nature expressed itself in a whole literature of adventure, natural and supernatural, in which a quasi-religious enthusiasm was applied to the results of modern technology. From Jules Verne's *20,000 Leagues Under the Sea* (1870) to H. G. Wells's *The First Men in the Moon* (1901), pre-Freudian fancies allied the technical agility of Victor Hugo's "industrial future" to a depth and assurance of belief which were the equivalent of his "religious past."

Art was slower to adapt itself, and for a good reason. In an age of great storytellers—perhaps the last great age, in fact, of the printed narrative—there was not much for art to do in that domain. Art's traditional subjects were far from exhausted when Jules Verne was at the height of his powers. Between 1880 and 1914 the waking life provided quite enough material for the constructive imagination of a Cézanne or a Matisse to get to work on. But when life began to patch itself together again after the end of World War I there was a case for saying that new art must fulfill new needs, and that the most urgent of new needs was to find ways of dealing with the liberated unconscious.

THE MANDATE OF SURREALISM

It was in response to this imperative that Surrealism came into being. The role of the Surrealists was to go where almost no one had gone before: to disentangle the dream and to present it—"infantile, grotesque or immoral as it may be"—complete and unaltered. The spokesmen for Surrealism were frankly and markedly imperialistic, in that they annexed terrain to which they had no exclusive right and dismissed, unheard, arguments of great weight and cogency. Paintings and sculptures which were not Surrealist in their allegiance were derided as sterile, outmoded, timid and effete. The dream was *everything* at that time. After 50 years we can see that a bathroom scene by Bonnard or an abstract painting by Mondrian was every bit as much of an imaginative achievement as any of the masterpieces of Surrealism. But at the time preconscious fancies stood on their own as the new subject matter of art, and he who was not with the Surrealists was against them. The dream *was* the imagination: or was at any rate the imagination's only rightful outlet. The sense of life stilled and suspended had always been present in art, and sometimes it had come out with a particular radiant gravity in parts of the world which could strictly have been called provincial—what better ex-

4. Max Klinger
The Glove, No. 7: "The Nightmare," 1878–80
The Museum of Modern Art, New York

That inanimate objects should take on a life of their own is fundamental to the dream. Max Klinger's series of etchings on the adventures and misadventures of a glove is a pioneer classic of its kind. The glove itself was to recur (fig. 6) in at least one major painting by de Chirico.

5. Edwin Romanzo Elmer
Mourning Picture, c. 1889
Smith College Museum of Art, Northampton, Mass.

II. Max Ernst
Pietà or Revolution by Night, 1923
Private collection, Turin

Elements of the Deposition, familiar to all
students of Old Master painting, are here
allied to the purest irrationality—and to an
echo of de Chirico in the downturned glance
and sober mien of the man in the derby hat.

III. René Magritte
The Menaced Assassin, 1926
The Museum of Modern Art, New York

Magritte had shelf upon shelf of detective stories at home, but there is no element of traditional mystery or detection in this painting. The circumspect assassin is surrounded on three sides, as he listens to the gramophone, by men who are determined either to club him down, or to catch him in a fishing net, or simply to make sure that he does not escape through the window. Meanwhile his victim lies, unheeded, on the sofa.

ample than the *Mourning Picture* (fig. 5) which was painted in the late 1880s by a little-known American, Edwin Romanzo Elmer?—but in the 1920s a small group of gifted people suddenly put forward the idea that this was the thing, and the only thing, on which the dignity of art would thereafter depend.

Like the earlier confederation of the dream of which I have just spoken, this one was international. Its most conspicuous members were Max Ernst, a German; Jean Arp, an Alsatian; Joan Miró, a Spaniard; André Masson, a Frenchman; René Magritte, a Belgian; Man Ray, an American; Alberto Giacometti, a Swiss; and Salvador Dali, another Spaniard. Insofar as they had a joint ancestor, he was Giorgio de Chirico, an Italian born in Greece. Most of the masterpieces of Surrealism were made in Paris, but the Surrealists did not rely, as Cézanne and Matisse had relied, on the almost unbroken evolutionary thrust of French painting as it had existed for several hundreds of years. Their allegiances derived from literature, from medicine, from psychoanalysis, and from the ideology of political revolution. "Beauty must be convulsive," wrote their chief spokesman, the poet and critic André Breton, "or it will cease to be."

Because Surrealism overlapped with the last days of Dada, and because some of the same people took part in both, it is clearly convenient to treat the one as the outcome of the other. But the truth is that they have almost nothing in common. In the First Surrealist Manifesto as it was published by Breton in 1924 there was none of that hostility to the past, that wish to ignore or abolish "art" and "literature" as they had previously existed, which was basic to Dada. Surrealism was fundamentally the continuation by other means of activities which could be traced back to the late 18th century. In 1936 when Breton was invited to introduce Surrealism to an English audience, he traced its origins to the summer of 1764, when Horace Walpole wrote his novel, *The Castle of Otranto,* under the influence of a dream in which he found himself on the great staircase of an ancient castle and saw on the topmost banister "a gigantic hand in armor." Walpole went on, "In the evening I sat down and began to write, without knowing in the least what I wanted to say or relate." In this way there was initiated the idea that Surrealism had one foot in automatism and the other in the dream.

Another English novel, Charles Maturin's *Melmoth the Wanderer* (1820), was among the ancestors of the book which is most often quoted in connection with the methodology of Surrealism. Maturin's demonic adventurer found his French counterpart in *Les Chants de Maldoror,* which was written in Paris in 1868 at the age of 22 by Isidore Ducasse, self-styled comte de Lautréamont. The key passage in this context is one in which Lautréamont

speaks of a 16-year-old English boy as being "as beautiful as the chance meeting on a dissecting table of a sewing machine and an umbrella." The famous passage is very much stronger, in point of fact, if it is read in full. We need, for instance, the image of the deserted Paris street along which the boy is walking while overhead "a screech-owl with a broken leg flies dead straight above the Madeleine"; and we also need the crescendo of oddity by which the boy's beauty has already been likened to "the retractility of the claws of birds of prey," to the specific effects of "wounds in the soft parts of the lower cervical region," and to the mechanism of a self-operating rat trap. But even in its diminished form the phrase upholds that fundamental principle of Surrealism by which seemingly unrelated objects turn out, when set side by side, to have an unexpected significance. The umbrella, the sewing machine and the dissecting table symbolize the improbable encounters in inappropriate places that can play so decisive a role in human life; and when André Breton wanted to justify the picturing of such encounters it was Edgar Allan Poe whom he called in as chief witness. Poe had written in his *Marginalia* that "the pure imagination chooses from either Beauty or Deformity only the most combinable things hitherto uncombined." He went on, "As so often happens in physical chemistry, so not unfrequently does it occur in the chemistry of the intellect that the admixture of two elements results in something that has nothing of the qualities of one of them, or even nothing of the qualities of either."

DE CHIRICO AND THE METAPHYSICAL OBJECT

Reactions of this kind had been set up in painting since 1911 by Giorgio de Chirico. The paintings in question were first exhibited in Paris before 1914, and Apollinaire for one got the point of them immediately. De Chirico became a familiar though quietly mutinous attender at Apollinaire's weekly receptions, and before long he assumed a place which he has never lost: that of the acknowledged forerunner of the new visionary painting. There was something almost supernatural about the initiatory powers which his work seemed to possess, and about the seemingly accidental ways in which it imposed itself on those who were predestined to make use of it. Breton first saw it in a shop window, Max Ernst in a bookshop in Munich, Yves Tanguy from the top of a bus, René Magritte when a friend chanced to show him a reproduction of the *Song of Love* (fig. 6). These were "chance encounters," but each came at a moment of maximum need for the artists in question.

We can still see why this was. A de Chirico of the period 1911–17 gives classic and definitive expression to anxieties char-

6. Giorgio de Chirico
Song of Love, 1914
Private collection, New York

With its unexpected jumps in scale, its backward glance at antiquity, its
unfathomable architecture, its locomotive with a head of steam up and its
bizarre conjunction of unrelated objects, de Chirico's *Song of Love* is one of
the representative masterpieces of our century.

7. Giorgio de Chirico
The Evil Genius of a King,
 1914–15
The Museum of Modern Art,
 New York

8. Giorgio de Chirico
The Child's Brain, 1914
Nationalmuseum, Stockholm

The Child's Brain hung for
many years in André Breton's
apartment in Paris, where it
became a key image for the
Surrealists.

acteristic of our century. Such has been the proliferation of the
image over the last 80 years that we have to apply to every new
work of art a terrible question: "Who needs it?" Only if the
answer is "Everybody" do we accept the work unreservedly; and
I hope to make it clear that in the case of a de Chirico of those
years we can still return that answer.

If these pictures make so much of Surrealism look feeble, con-
trived, or superfluous it is partly because de Chirico set himself
so stringent a criterion. It was that the basic idea of each painting
must give the painter "such joy or such pain that he has no alternative but to paint it and is driven on by a force greater even than
that which drives a starving man to bite into the first piece of

9. Giorgio de Chirico
The Philosopher's Conquest, 1914
The Art Institute of Chicago

The belching factory chimney, the symbols of imminent departure (locomotive and sailing ship), the phallic artillery with its accompaniment of two huge balls, the mysterious cowled figures whose shadows appear beneath the clock—all these make *The Philosopher's Conquest* one of the most dense, as well as one of the most cryptic, of de Chirico's paintings.

10. Giorgio de Chirico
The Mathematicians, 1917
The Museum of Modern Art,
New York

In this drawing de Chirico blurred the distinction between a human being and a piece of furniture in ways that Picasso, for one, was to take up many years later in an etching (fig. 31) from the Vollard suite.

bread that comes his way." The observer must identify, equally, with the first man in the world, "who must have seen auguries everywhere, and trembled with every step that he took."

De Chirico had a very low opinion of the accredited Surrealists when they eventually materialized, and there is nothing in his work of the invalidish imaginings which run wild in Lautréamont. His compound images derive from identifiable elements in his own life, even if they have been edited and recombined in ways for which "dreamlike" is as good a word as any. He had also looked with great intelligence both at the union of disparate elements in the pasted-paper works of Picasso and Braque and at the use of flat silhouette in Synthetic Cubism; these helped him to present his ideas with a measured coherence and a logic that was not of the waking world.

He did not wait in passivity for the dream to put subjects in his way. "The methods of people like Thomas de Quincey do not tempt us," he wrote in 1919. He saw the artist as someone who used the gift of clairvoyance to reappraise the objects of everyday, and to release from within them a mysterious and ominous element which normally passes unnoticed. "Metaphysical" was the name which he gave to this element. "We who know the signs of the metaphysical alphabet," he went on, "are aware of the joy and the solitude which are enclosed by a portico, by the corner of a street, or even in a room, on the surface of a table, or between the sides of a box. . . . The minutely accurate and prudently weighed use of surfaces and volumes constitutes the canon of the metaphysical aesthetic." De Chirico had a pan-European inheritance, and his education was as much German as Italian; in his student days in Munich he had learned from Schopenhauer that "to have original, extraordinary and perhaps even immortal ideas one has only to isolate oneself from the world for a few moments in such a way that even the most commonplace happenings seem new and unfamiliar, and so reveal their true essence."

He remained loyal to this idea: "The daemon in everything must be discovered." Sometimes it was enough simply to displace an object from the environment in which we expect to see it, "like an armchair, a divan and some chairs, grouped together on the traditionless prairies of distant America." Sometimes a change of scale did the trick, as when he noticed how, outside a little workshop in a Parisian side street, "a huge glove made of painted zinc, with terrible gilded nails, was pointing with its index finger at the stones of the sidewalk." Sometimes the image was carried forward like a mascot from his childhood: a huge and archaic cannon, for instance, which he remembered from the harbor in Volos, the Greek seaport where he had first been brought up. Sometimes he stayed even nearer to the facts of his youth. His father had been a railway engineer; and the town terminal, the station clock and the locomotive with its plumes of steam were early members of the "metaphysical alphabet." Sometimes he drew upon the grander, more spacious elements of Greek or Italian town planning, sometimes on specific works of ancient art (notably an antique statue of Ariadne), sometimes on fragments of the Italian industrial scene: factory chimneys above all. A tireless window shopper, he found metaphysics in the shapes of the biscuits put out by specialized pastrycooks and metaphysics again in the relief maps of Europe which were in vogue after the outbreak of World War I.

Where other painters strove for infinity with pictures of mountain ranges and distant horizons, de Chirico from 1914 onward worked intensively on what he called "the terribleness of lines and angles," bringing his subject matter close to the picture plane in Cubist style and inducing in the observer a systematic disorientation. He did nothing that was not personal to himself; yet the result has a universal resonance, and we can agree with what de Chirico said of it in 1919—that it arose from "a fatality of the human spirit which is governed by fixed mathematical laws. It ebbs, flows, departs, returns and is reborn like everything else on our planet."

A MYTHOLOGY FOR MODERN TIMES

Giorgio de Chirico invented as valid a metaphor as painting has to show for the anxiety, the sense of unfocused guilt and dread, which has been common to almost every thinking individual throughout the 20th century. In his world nothing is what it seems; our relationship to our environment is warped at every turn; normal life is suspended. Omens are everywhere: we cannot see the little girl bowling her hoop in *The Mystery and Melancholy of a Street* (fig. 13) without being reminded by her two-dimensional silhouette of how running figures were turned into flattened and calcinated profiles when Dresden was destroyed by fire in 1945.

What de Chirico did, between 1911 and 1917, was to create a modern mythology—a compound of private guilt and the externals of big-city life—which has never been superseded. Proud and resentful by nature, he did not at all care for the interpretation which was put upon his work in Paris from 1914 onward. First Apollinaire, and in later years André Breton, had major paintings by de Chirico in their apartments; in both cases the pictures were used as a point of departure for the poetics of free association. But whereas de Chirico distinguished sharply between the climate of the dream and the dream itself, Breton and his friends identified the cult of the dream with the cult of psychic automatism. "I define Surrealism once and for all," Breton wrote in the First Surrealist Manifesto, "as that pure psychic automatism by which we propose to express, whether in speech, on the printed page, or by any other means, the true functioning of thought. Whatever thought dictates to us is to be immune from conscious control by our reason and shall be set down without regard either for aesthetics or for morality. Surrealism is based on a belief in the superior reality of certain hitherto neglected forms of association, in the supreme authority of the dream, and in the disinterested play of the thought processes."

It sounded categorical enough. And it did, in point of fact, apply to the experiments in automatic writing which Breton and his friends had been making. Other, earlier precedents in literature were adduced by Breton: the state of "supernaturalist revery," for instance, in which the poet Gérard de Nerval (1808–1855) claimed to have written a series of sonnets. If no such precedents were brought forward in art it was because art had, in Breton's view, lagged behind. "It is preposterous," he wrote some years later, "that drawing and painting should still stand today at the point at which writing stood before Gutenberg." But there was not in 1924 a body of work which could be discussed in terms of the "internal model" which was to apotheosize the role of the dream in human affairs. By 1928, when Breton for the

11. Carlo Carrà
Metaphysical Muse, 1917
Emilio Jesi, Milan

Something of de Chirico's vocabulary—his menacing way with architecture,
his delight in relief maps, his ability to see the human body half as a lay figure,
half as automaton—was taken up in 1917 by the Futurist painter Carlo Carrà
in his *Metaphysical Muse.* The painting is, moreover, an anthology of themes
which were to preoccupy other artists many years later: the target (Kenneth
Noland and Jasper Johns), the map (Johns, once again), and the summary,
schematic automaton (Oskar Schlemmer in the 1920s).

12. George Grosz
Republican Automatons, 1920
The Museum of Modern Art, New York

After World War I George Grosz exploited elements from de Chirico's
vocabulary to press home a satirical point about the people who had served like
robots in the German Army and lost no time in adapting themselves to a
change of political regime.

first time wrote specifically on Surrealism and painting, he was able to present not only de Chirico but Max Ernst, Joan Miró, André Masson and Yves Tanguy as committed Surrealists. Over the next year or two René Magritte, Salvador Dali and Alberto Giacometti came along to complete what was by any count a body of very substantial artists. But in 1924 Max Ernst was the only person who had consistently followed de Chirico's lead in producing images which effected "a meeting of two distant realities on a plane foreign to them both"; and as he made many of these under the aegis of Dada (and at times under the name of "Dadamax") it got to be taken for granted that Dada overlapped into Surrealism and had much the same base.

This is true on a personal level, and it was partly true on the level of literature. Breton was anxious to annex for Surrealism the things that he admired in Dada; when outflanked in that intention he put it about that Dada had died in the spring of 1921, in any case, and that "for a long time now, the risks have been taken elsewhere." The fact that many people concerned remained the same made it even more natural to smudge history; but the differences between Dada art and Surrealist art are fundamental enough to be worth defining here.

Dada was an emergency operation. Based on an economy of starvation and on the total rejection of the past, it was international and even intercontinental in its development. It responded to a situation in which the end of the world as it had previously existed for art could reasonably be regarded as imminent. In such a situation, ad hoc materials alone were appropriate. Surrealism was hardly less radical in its program; but, in spite of that, Surrealist art was largely a matter of old-style paintings on canvas which were put on offer in old-style galleries in a world bent on "going back to normal." It is also pertinent that Dada was opposed to the very idea of "a career in art" and that with one or two exceptions the Dadaists were not people whose gifts would support a long lifetime of continuous effort. With Miró, Ernst, Magritte and Giacometti—to name four only—the case was quite different; and during the years from 1917 to 1921 Miró as a very young man was painting pictures of a fulfilled and completely energized sort which were the antithesis of Dada and could be said to have guaranteed, on their own, a great future for painting.

André Breton was by origin a man of letters, and in 1921 he was still fundamentally the young man who had come to Paris on leave from the French Army in 1916 and made a name for himself by reason of his extreme beauty of person ("archangelical" was the adjective most in favor for this), his precocious gifts as a poet, and the frenzy of excitement and awe in which he presented himself to the writers whom he most admired. Breton had

13. Giorgio de Chirico
The Mystery and Melancholy of a Street, 1914
Mr. and Mrs. Stanley S. Resor, New Canaan, Conn.

that same effect upon others in later life; but it came to be overlooked that at the age of 18 he had written a sonnet which drew from Paul Valéry, a great poet 25 years his senior, the rueful admission that in Breton's lines he heard a language which he himself no longer knew how to speak.

Breton always remembered the exact moment at which the image began to rank equal, in his eyes, with the written word. It was early in 1921, at Picabia's house in Paris. Breton was there with the poet and novelist Louis Aragon, the poet Philippe Soupault, and Tristan Tzara, the veteran of international Dada, when

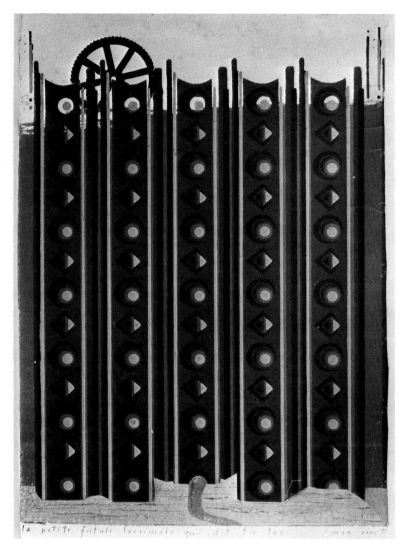

la petite fistule lacrimale qui dit tic tac

14. Max Ernst
The Little Tear Gland That Says Tic Tac, 1920
The Museum of Modern Art, New York

With a piece of wallpaper, a cogwheel from a manual of engineering and a hand-painted flow of heavy, viscous liquid, Max Ernst produced what is both an odd image in itself and a sly commentary on the machinery by which our inmost feelings make themselves visible.

the mailman delivered a package from Cologne. Inside it were the collages which Max Ernst was to show in Paris. "They introduced," Breton wrote, "an entirely original scheme of visual structure; yet they corresponded exactly to the intentions of Lautréamont and Rimbaud in poetry. . . . We were all filled immediately with unparalleled admiration. The external object had broken free from its normal environment, and its component parts had become emancipated from it in such a way as to maintain entirely new relationships with other elements in the collages."

Thereafter, Max Ernst was the test case, the exception to the rule, the man from out of town (he moved to Paris in 1922) who was manifestly as much at home in literature as he was in art. He was a poet among the poets, a painter among the painters, a prehensile many-sided inventor who gave art, in the eyes of the Surrealist writers, a fresh start and a prestige without precedent. There was nothing in his works, Breton said, which could not be found in the observer's own experience; yet they invalidated all our systems of reference, so that we could no longer find our way among our own memories.

In the work which Max Ernst showed in Paris in May, 1921, speed of wit was allied to speed of manufacture. He racked up in double time a whole dictionary of new technical possibilities for art. He was not "a natural painter," in the sense that Chardin or Manet or Braque was a natural painter. If he could elide, abbreviate, or with impunity miss ten turns in the long manual process of "painting a picture," he did so; what mattered was not the physical beauty of the thing done but the readiness—as Breton had noticed at once—to put our experience at risk.

Joan Miró did not in 1921 seem likely to rival Max Ernst in his mastery of dislocation. The son and grandson of Catalan craftsmen, Miró had had none of the intensive literary education which was common to both Ernst and Breton. Nor was he familiar, as they were, with the development of abnormal psychology. But as a student in Barcelona during World War I he had seen a majestic survey of recent French painting which had been chosen by Ambroise Vollard and sent to Barcelona. Among wartime visitors to that delectable city he had met Picabia in 1917 and the French poet Pierre Reverdy, who was a lifelong friend of Braque. He had also seen the Ballets Russes which Diaghilev had brought to Barcelona. All this had helped to de-provincialize him; and as he combined an appetite for the new with an inherited command of robust craftsmanship, it came about between 1917 and 1921 that without ever having been to Paris he produced painting after painting which amounted to, in effect, an inspired critique of the state of French art.

15. Max Ernst
All Friends Together, 1922
Wallraf-Richartz-Museum, Cologne

Friends and allies, real or imaginary, true or false, are here combined in a group portrait. Max Ernst sits on Dostoevsky's knee, Raphael makes an unexpected appearance in the background, fellow artists include de Chirico and Arp, and there is a strong representation of French poets and men of letters: among them Aragon, Breton, Paul Eluard, Robert Desnos and Benjamin Péret. The bizarre hand movements relate to the sign language of the deaf and dumb.

His *Portrait of E. C. Ricart,* 1917 (fig. 17), was, for instance, an appendix to the enthusiasm for the Japanese print which infected one major artist after another from van Gogh to Bonnard. His *Portrait of a Woman* of 1918 (fig. 18) came near to Matisse in its presentation of a firmly modeled human body against a background and floor-ground of vivid allover patterning. No account of Fauvism is complete without some reference to the riot of color which characterizes the landscapes which Miró painted at Montroig not far from Barcelona in 1919. *Table with Glove* of 1921 (fig. 19) is as remarkable as Picasso's great *Still Life with Bread and Fruitdish* of 1909 (Volume 4) for its mingling of up-to-date formal devices with the extreme solidity of traditional Spanish still life. This was painting of a class which did not need to look beyond itself for its justification. Still less did it need to sign a treaty of alliance with the printed word. An extreme particularity of vision—the power to identify strongly and in turn with every object in the picture—is allied in paintings like *Table with Glove* to rock-steady compositional powers; the result is an icon of stability.

Yet within a year of his first sojourn in Paris Miró was painting in a completely different and new way. Familiar images, released from the solid architectural schema of the earlier paintings, raced helter-skelter across the canvas; concurrently, a free-running fantasy brought with it an atmosphere of carnival in which it seemed quite natural for a lizard in a wizard's cap to break off his reading of the newspaper to start a conversation with a snail. Whereas in 1917 Miró tilled every inch of the picture as carefully as the Catalan farmer tills his red earth, by 1923 he was treating the

16. Joan Miró
View of Montroig, 1917
The Solomon R. Guggenheim Museum, New York

17. Joan Miró
Portrait of E. C. Ricart (called *The Man in Pyjamas*), 1917
The Museum of Modern Art, New York

18. Joan Miró
Portrait of a Woman, 1918
The Art Institute of Chicago

20. Joan Miró
The Table (Still Life with Rabbit), 1920
Gustav Zumsteg, Zürich

19. Joan Miró
Table with Glove, 1921
The Museum of Modern Art, New York

In the winter of 1921 Miró rented a studio in Paris that was virtually unheated. Many years later he recounted that the fur-lined glove in this painting was so stiff from the cold that it retained the shape of his hand and was put into the picture as a sign of his own presence.

canvas as a blank space on which to rough out his thoughts in diagrammatic style and according to a shorthand of his own devising. Heads in that shorthand were transparent and triangular; hearts were shown as ticking bombs; and a rifle at the ready became a tall thin black cone with a flame at the top of it. Where Matisse in his *Joy of Life* (Volume 2) had included a faithful representation of a Catalan round-dance called the *sardana*, Miró in his *The Hunter (Catalan Landscape)* of 1923–24 (fig. 23) simply wrote in the first four letters of its name in the corner. He then left it to us to work out whether he was thinking of the SARDana

21. Joan Miró
The Tilled Field, 1923–24
The Solomon R. Guggenheim Museum,
New York

or, no less plausibly, about the SARDine which, fresh and lightly grilled, is a great delicacy in that part of Spain.

Miró from his beginnings had subjected every object in his paintings to that penetrating scrutiny which is traditional to the Spanish *bodegon,* or still life. He could not paint so much as a watering can or a pair of steps, let alone a dead rabbit, without giving it an animistic intensity; and as early as 1917 he had invented an ideogram of brightly colored stripes to stand for a ploughed field. In the early 1920s he went one step further—just one, but a big one—in the direction of a purely poetic evocation. He still regarded his landscapes as realistic—"more essentially Montroig," he said later, "than if they had been painted from nature"—but he no longer thought of painting as an ambition complete in itself. His new friends in Paris, and above all his neighbor André Masson, taught him to think of the act of representing the everyday world as something subordinate and transi-

tional; the role of the true artist was to go beyond painting. ("Beyond Painting" is, by the way, the title of an important essay by Max Ernst.) The artist's activity should be what we now call trans- or interdisciplinary; he was there not to *represent* the ideas that came to him but to *list* them, uncensored. By bringing into the open what is most often bundled out of the way he would resite the locus of human uncertainty and put it where it belonged: in the unconscious.

One of the things that Miró did was to carry over into painting the idea of automatic writing. Many of his paintings from 1923 onward were as much written as painted: sometimes literally, in that handwritten texts were an important part of the picture's formal constituents, and sometimes metaphorically, in that the forms in a picture like his *Carnival of Harlequin* (fig. 22) were noted down individually and in terms of condensed biomorphic symbols. (Something in those lollopy biomorphic signs was owed

IV. Joan Miró
The Birth of the World, 1925
The Museum of Modern Art, New York

The Birth of the World was until 1968 one of the unknown masterpieces of modern art. Like Picasso's *Les Demoiselles d'Avignon* (Volume 4) and Matisse's *The Moroccans,* it went unseen for many years. Its radical nature lay in the combination of automatic or purely inspirational drawing with thinned-out paint that was spilled, blotted or brushed loosely and allowed to run free. What was being born was not so much "the world"—though the total image could be related to the first stumblings of creativity—as a new kind of painting: one that for the first time got clear away both from the tight scaffolding and shallow space of Cubism and the illusionistic naturalism of first-generation Surrealist painting. Miró aimed at what he called "an unlimited atmospheric space," as against the limitations of perspective or the confining grid of Cubism. The canvas was prepared in such a way that accident and irregularity were built into it from the start. Incidents of this sort were worked up by Miró into the elements of a new universe: a shooting star, a bird, a man. What he produced was not "order out of chaos" but a meaningful chaos out of an unmeaningful one; in doing so, he stored up for later painters a whole new picture language— free, informal, as independent of distance as of gravity. *The Birth of the World* signaled the rebirth of painting as it occurred from the mid-1940s onward.

19

22. Joan Miró
Carnival of Harlequin,
1924–25
Albright-Knox Art Gallery,
Buffalo, N.Y.

23. Joan Miró
The Hunter (Catalan Landscape), 1923–24
The Museum of Modern Art, New York

Miró had always drawn his inspiration from the landscape, the people, the
climate and the produce of his native Catalonia. He was still doing it in this at
first sight somewhat cryptic painting. William Rubin lately identified no fewer
than 58 specific local references in what is basically "an image of a peasant
hunting in the Catalan countryside." It is, however, a deft mingling of factual
references (the hunter has a mustache and a beard, smokes a pipe, and wears
an identifiable kind of local cap) with elements of pure fantasy: "monstrous
animals and angelic animals," as Miró wrote at the time, "and trees with ears
and eyes."

20

to Arp, who lived in the same house as Miró at the time.) Miró said in 1933 that his work was "always born in a state of hallucination due to a shock of some kind—subjective or objective—for which I bear no responsibility." In other words, he switched off the conscious mind and just let the images come: initially under the pressures of hunger, later as the result of a faculty by then well developed. This is, of course, a grossly simplified account of what must always have been a complex, intermittent and often self-contradictory process. It takes time to make a picture, even if the means employed are as summary as those of the *Spanish Dancer* of 1928; and although the notion of total automatism can be upheld as a philosophical position it is difficult not to believe that automatism is more effective when used as a booster, or as a form of overdrive, than when the artist allows it complete command of his actions. What passes for successful automatism may result from a dis-inhibited fancy, an original gift for metaphor, and the ability to move forward from "painting," as hitherto understood, to an amalgam of painting and object making. A signal instance of this is Miró's *The Writer,* which dates from the crucial year 1924 and is at once a portrait (of Apollinaire, according to the interpretation of Margit Rowell), a list of the writer's materials, a list of the vowels at his disposal, and (by virtue of the two postage stamps in the upper right corner) a demonstration of what it can all amount to: a letter ready for mailing. Hallucinatory it may have been, in its origins; but there is too much in the way of wit and allusion (to Apollinaire's play *Les Mamelles de Tirésias,* in particular) to make us accept it as an unaltered message from the unconscious.

When André Masson took André Breton to Miró's studio in 1924, Breton dismissed Miró's work as altogether too childlike. The pictures were daring, but they were not *seen* to be daring in terms of the iconography of panic which Breton was promoting. To the extent that the unconscious does not usually bring us good news, and that what we repress is hatred more often than love, Breton was right to prefer the dislocated images of Max Ernst (or, for that matter, the arrowy, allover, seemingly improvised drawings and paintings of Masson). Miró in 1924 still stuck to the traditions of easel painting, and to the logic of pictorial statement which he had learned from Cubism; and although he was to go far beyond this by 1927 it was Max Ernst, in 1924, who best fulfilled the Surrealists' mandate.

Ernst did it above all in the construction called *Two Children Are Threatened by a Nightingale* (pl. VI), which starts from one of those instincts of irrational panic which we suppress in our waking lives. Only in dreams can a diminutive songbird scare the daylights out of us; only in dreams can the button of an alarm bell swell to the size of a beach ball and yet remain just out of our reach. *Two Children* incorporates elements from traditional European painting: perspectives that give an illusion of depth, a subtly atmospheric sky, formalized poses that come straight from the Old Masters, a distant architecture of dome and tower and triumphal arch. But it also breaks out of the frame, in literal terms: the alarm or doorbell, the swinging gate on its hinge, and the blind-walled house are three-dimensional constructions, physical objects in the real world. We are both in, and out of, painting; in, and out of, art; in, and out of, a world subject to rational interpretation. Where traditional painting subdues disbelief by presenting us with a world unified on its own terms, Max Ernst in the *Two Children* breaks the contract over and over again. We have reason to disbelieve the plight of his two children. Implausible in itself, it is set out in terms which eddy between those of fine art and those of the toyshop. Nothing "makes sense" in the picture. Yet the total experience is undeniably meaningful; Ernst has recreated a sensation painfully familiar to us from our dreams but never before quite recaptured in art—that of total disorientation in a world where nothing keeps to its expected scale or fulfills its expected function.

In principle, the entire terrain of human experience was open to the Surrealists, yet what actually happened was far more restricted in its implications. Surrealism as sponsored by André Breton was predominantly Freudian in its allegiances; and like much of what Freud wrote it was founded on a patient replay of childhood experience. Above all, Surrealism was about the overthrow of authority, and more especially about the overthrow of authority as represented by the father. De Chirico was haunted by the withdrawn, authoritarian figure of his father. Max Ernst was marked for life by the imperious rhythm of childbearing which his father imposed on his mother, and by the hallucinatory intimations of this which came to him in dreams. Fathers in general stood for authority, for repression, for conjugal rights exercised with a brutish regularity; and the Surrealists turned with a particular ferocity on public men whose activity seemed to them to be paternalist in character. One such was Paul Claudel, the playwright and poet who for many years held high rank in the French diplomatic service. Claudel was strong on duty, strong on obedience, strong on the letter of the law. He would have been anathema to the Surrealists even if in 1925 he had not been imprudent enough to say that "neither Dada nor Surrealism can lead to anything new; they are for pederasts only." The Surrealists replied with a long collective letter that ended, "we ask for ourselves the 'dishonor' of having treated you once and for all as the trash that you are." Claudel deserved it; but the riposte was

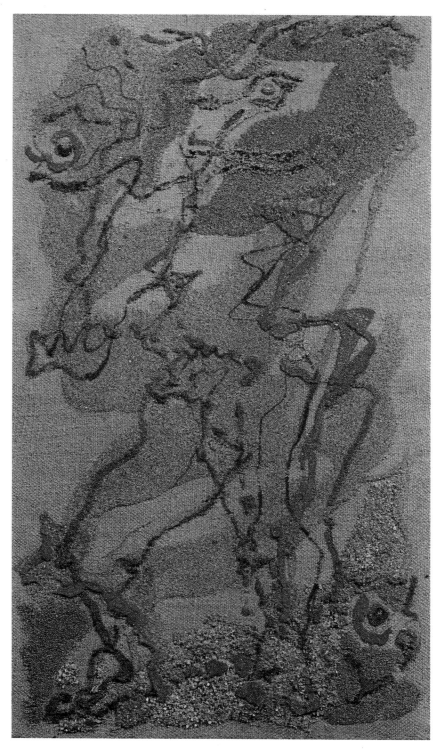

V. André Masson
Painting (Figure), 1927
The Museum of Modern Art, New York

Inventive in all things, André Masson was one of the first to experiment
with textures which departed entirely from those traditional to fine art.
Here he uses sand, in combination with vigorous freehand drawing,
to produce an image that still has a hallucinatory quality.

2 enfants sont menacés par un rossignol /M. ernst

VI. Max Ernst
*Two Children Are Threatened by
    a Nightingale,* 1924
The Museum of Modern Art, New York

In this disquieting little work Ernst
brings out several classic aspects of the
dream. Its disproportions, for instance:
there is something quite irrational
about the size of the alarm or doorbell
which the man on the roof is so
desperately trying to reach. And its
mingling of exact realism with a most
lunatic exaggeration: who was ever
frightened by a nightingale, anyway?
Ernst also pioneered the combination of
objects from real life—such as the
model picket fence—with painstaking
passages of painted illusion, like the
traditional perspective which forces the
exotic architecture into a simulated
far distance.

23

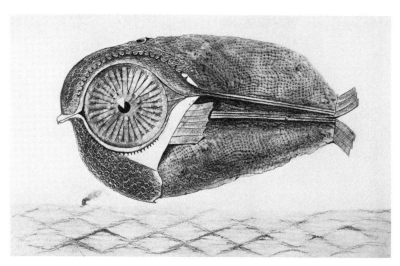

24. Max Ernst
Sheet from *Histoire Naturelle*, 1926
The Museum of Modern Art, New York

Max Ernst began his *Histoire Naturelle* with chance impressions dictated, so he said, by the graining on the floor of a country hotel. Be that as it may, he soon worked it up into strange images which combine shreds and slivers of natural history with a demonic gift for the invention of new creatures, new landscapes, and new metaphors for universal human predicaments.

addressed as much to the institution of fatherhood as to the pre-potent rhetorician, then in the prime of life, who was the French ambassador in Tokyo.

Art was, in such contexts, the best possible way of paying off old scores. Oedipal feelings ran berserk throughout the 1920s. Imaginary misfortunes were constantly being wished on the representatives of fatherhood, and not least on God the Father himself. The prototypical Surrealist title is *Mama, Papa Is Wounded!* (pl. VIII), and it would stick in our minds even if the painting in question (by Yves Tanguy) were not one of the finest of its date. Salvador Dali returned over and over again to the image of the son castrated by his father. The father, everywhere, was seen as having done his son an irreparable mischief; and his presence, whether in de Chirico's *The Child's Brain* (fig. 8) or in Max Ernst's *Pietà or Revolution by Night* (pl. II) or in one of their many derivatives, was seen as granitic, oppressive, unyielding.

THE RESTATEMENT OF THE RIGHTS OF MAN

As a comment on intergenerational hostility, these things were memorably vivid. Insofar as several of the artists concerned did genuinely still bear the wounds of childhood, the works in question had an immediacy which can no longer be recaptured. The mid-1920s were the first moment in time at which it was possible for an artist to interpret his early experience in the light of psychoanalysis: they were also the last moment in time at which this could count as authentic pioneering. On a more general and less private level many taboos which now seem to us impossibly archaic were then still taken for granted.

Surrealism stood in all this for the restatement of the rights of man. Breton had always in his mind what he called "the future continent": a landmass, as yet unlocated, on which all men would tread freely and as equals. All women, too: many years before Women's Liberation was heard of, Breton laid it down as an integral part of Surrealism that "not only must we put an end to the exploitation of men by other men, but we must review—from top to bottom, in a totally unhypocritical spirit and as a matter of the first urgency—the problem of men's relations with women." In this, the Surrealists ranged themselves behind Charles Fourier (1772–1837), the Utopian socialist, who said that the essential prerequisite for social change was that women should be free to dispose of themselves as independent human beings.

The masterpieces of Surrealism have long ago been tamed and ticketed. But it is still very well worthwhile to look at them in the light of what the English historian G. M. Young once had to say about the writing of history. "The real central theme of history," he said, "is not what happened but what people felt about it when it was happening." Time and the museums combine to flatten what was for the artist and his contemporaries the most urgent aspect of his work: its either/or quality. For those who live by them, beliefs are nonetheless tenacious for being unfounded. It seemed to the Surrealists that there was, for instance, a straight choice, a clear-cut either/or, between the liberated imagination and the drudgery of copying appearances; a straight choice between liberated sexuality and the shams and compromises authorized by society; and a straight choice between the steeple-chase of image and idea which the Surrealists had in mind and the predictable manufacturing of standard subject paintings which was to turn much of French painting into a sub-department of the souvenir trade.

In all this the truth was bent, much as it is bent in time of war when the overriding consideration is to keep the reader, or the listener, in good heart. Time sorts all things out: and time has

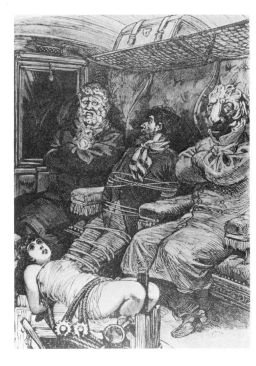 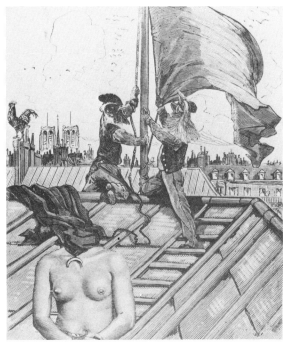 

25. Max Ernst
Three pages from *Une Semaine de bonté* (a book of engravings in 5 volumes)
Editions Jeanne Bucher, Paris, 1934

Under its ironical title, *A Week of Loving Kindness,* the collage-novel *Une Semaine de bonté* is filled with compound images of terror, violence, misfortune and loss. A fiery and athletic imagination is here seen at full stretch (the entire book was completed in three weeks) and page after page has a premonitory power: the imminent collapse of European civilization is prefigured over and over again.

already told us that the dosage of poetic imagination in a great Matisse is as high as in the finest of Surrealist paintings; that the sexual content of Ingres and Courbet has as much weight and resource as can be found anywhere in Surrealism; and that it was not the Surrealists but Mondrian, with his search for a constructive and immutable truth, who put forward the most audacious alternative to traditional painting in the 1920s. But this is quite immaterial: artists believe what they have to believe, and in the 1920s and '30s this was as true of the private domain—the management of their own gifts, that is to say—as it was in matters of universal principle. Max Ernst had so strong a creative identity that whatever he did was distinctly his own, even if it began from the automatic imprint of a piece of graining on the floorboards of a country hotel. What resulted was specifically, unmistakably, peremptorily his own. But when he was asked to define Surrealism in 1934 he said that there was no such thing as individual talent, and that the legend of individual creativity was one of the last and most ridiculous of the superstitions with which the civilization of the Occident was encumbered. The active, constructive, initiatory role of the artist was a myth; all that he had to do in reality was to open the doors of the unconscious and play host to the inexhaustible stock of images which would come flooding in.

That was, and is still, the dialectical position of the Surrealists. Talented people can afford to place a taboo on the name of talent, since they know perfectly well that under one name or another their gifts will be acknowledged. But since the Surrealists were also very strong on the destruction of taboos it may well seem to us paradoxical that in this one context they were all for their re-erection. Apart from anything else it is simply not true that the stock of images which came flooding in from the liberated unconscious was inexhaustible. On the contrary: the repertory of images which each of the Surrealists had at his command is fundamentally quite small. What makes their work re-

25

VII. Max Ernst
The Angel of Hearth and Home, 1937
Private collection, Paris

Ernst is here at his most sardonic. Memories of childhood have combined with
more immediate distresses and exasperations to produce a sinister image of
what can lurk behind the façade of the sober and the settled life.

26

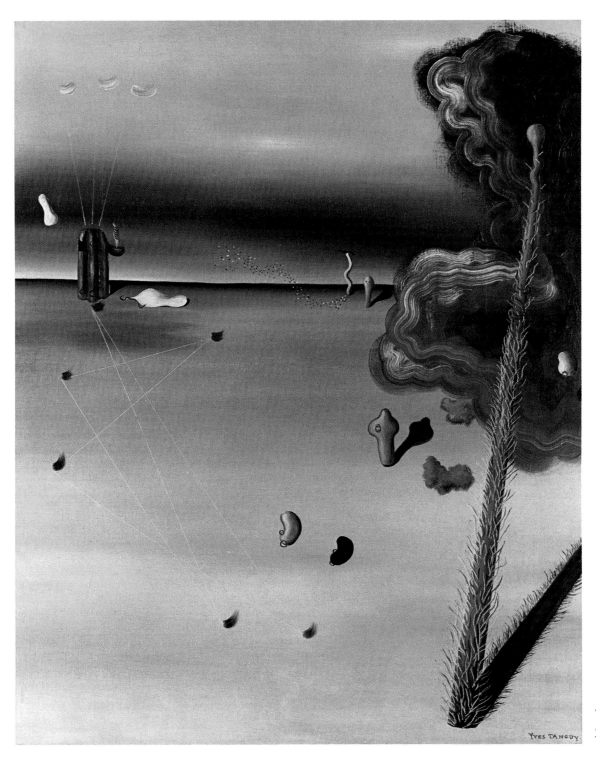

VIII. Yves Tanguy
Mama, Papa Is Wounded! 1927
The Museum of Modern Art, New York

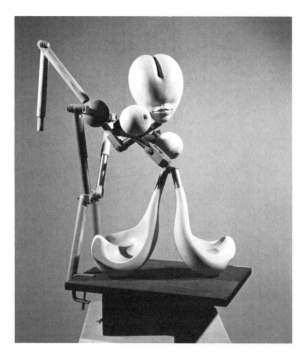

26. Hans Bellmer
Machinegun (La Mitrailleuse), 1937
The Museum of Modern Art, New York

The French word for machinegun is feminine in gender. Never one to pass up
an opportunity of that sort, Hans Bellmer was quick to invent a poetical object,
half woman and half instrument of aggression, which stood for femininity in
its voracious and destructive aspect.

27. Salvador Dali
The Birth of Liquid Desires, 1932
Peggy Guggenheim Foundation, Venice

28. Salvador Dali
Illumined Pleasures, 1929
The Museum of Modern Art, New York

In *Illumined Pleasures* Dali destroyed the unity of time, place and scale on
which earlier painting had depended. In their stead, he presents an anthology
of human enjoyments—some of them reputable, some of them not—in a
glassy, meticulous, illusionistic style which is intended to suspend disbelief
from the outset.

29. Salvador Dali
The Persistence of Memory,
1931
The Museum of Modern Art,
New York

The clock as tyrant was fundamental to many of de Chirico's best paintings. When Dali took over the notion of mechanized timekeeping he showed the watch as softened (and by implication, as emasculated). He hung it from the tree like laundry. He allowed it to hang down from the tablecloth like a used napkin. He draped it across the back of a nonexistent sea creature like a saddle that will never be needed. Time lost its terrors in a landscape which has itself proved immune to time: the rocky coast around Dali's home at Port Lligat in Spain.

markable is the resource, the energy, the deep feeling with which they deployed these images. The triumphs of individual talent are as clear, in Surrealism, as they are anywhere else; what is peculiar to Surrealism is the cruelty with which it points to individual shortcomings.

Surrealism always tended toward an iconography of disquiet. An art which is expressly anticonformist makes its point by sabotaging the existing order of things; and a free and open sexuality was intended to be the model, in this instance, for a free and open society. But the view of sexuality which actually came out in the work was, as often as not, pessimistic and incomplete, crippled and fearful. Breton wanted women to be in charge of their own destinies; but that same Breton was obsessed with the praying mantis—a species of insect where the female eats the male after he has satisfied her desires—to the point of rearing them in his own house and keeping them as pets. The image of Woman in Surrealism is predominantly that of a ravening monster: we need think only of the war dance of Ernst's *The Angel of Hearth and Home* (pl. VII); of Dali's vision of sex appeal in *Illumined Pleasures* (fig. 28) as an amalgam of terror and abnormality; of

30. Pablo Picasso
Seated Bather, 1930
The Museum of Modern Art, New York

Picasso here is working as a painter, but thinking as a sculptor. The carved and carpentered image of the seated woman is conceived in terms of opened-out forms which operate in three dimensions. The painting is also specifically Surrealist in the freedom with which Picasso puts forward the notion of woman as a devouring animal. The watchful, waiting bather is the personification of the female praying mantis, which eats its mate after lovemaking.

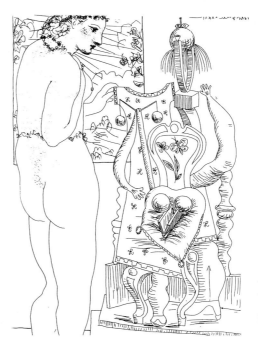

31. Pablo Picasso
Model and Surrealist Figure, 1933
From the Vollard suite of etchings

Picasso in 1933 was keenly interested in Surrealism, both for its own sake and as an activity on which he could make periodic and piratical raids. The "surrealist figure" which the beautiful girl is examining in this etching derives ultimately from the images (fig. 10) in which de Chirico reinvented the human body in terms of furniture; but Picasso's reinventions are more radical, and when it came to the erotic implications of the subject he allowed himself a caustic humor which was not in de Chirico's nature.

André Masson's *Landscape with Mantis,* and of Hans Bellmer's *Machinegun* (fig. 26), from which we can only infer that anyone who approaches the female sex is likely to be shot down or gobbled up as soon as he gets within reach. Fear dominated in all this; access to the unconscious has been bought at a very high price.

An iconography of disquiet, then; almost an iconography of doom. There were good reasons for this, both private and public. But there was also a generic reason and one which had been set out quite clearly many years before by Gustave Flaubert, the author of *Madame Bovary,* when he wrote that "the mental vision of the artist should not be regarded as equivalent to that of a man

IX. Joan Miró
Head of a Woman, 1938
The Minneapolis Institute of Arts

Miró was inspired by the outbreak of civil war in Spain to produce this painting, which would earn its place in any illustrated history of outrage. As much as Max Ernst's *The Angel of Hearth and Home* (pl. VII) it is a key image for the 1930s.

32. Max Ernst
The Big Forest, 1927
Kunstmuseum, Basel

Max Ernst was fascinated from childhood onward by the phenomenon of the forest: that vast, tangled, twilit arena from which so many German poets, composers, painters and storytellers have drawn their inspiration. In his hands it often took on, as here, a sinister connotation which was to reach its apotheosis in *Europe After the Rain* (fig. 36).

33. Meret Oppenheim
Object, 1936
The Museum of Modern Art, New York

In the chronology of Surrealism the Oppenheim teacup is a relatively late arrival. But it is the epitome of the Surrealist surprise: a self-contradictory object that defeats expectation at every turn. Taste, touch and sight are outraged by the idea of a cup that offers only fur when we raise it to our lips; yet the object itself haunts our imagination.

laboring under a hallucination. I know all that there is to know about both states, and an abyss separates one from the other. In hallucination, strictly so called, there is always an element of fear. You feel that you are losing your own personality and that you are on the point of death.''

Flaubert could not have foreseen how amply his opinion would be borne out by Surrealism. The Surrealists claimed for themselves a freedom of reference which had neither limit nor precedent. Yet there was as often as not something of defeatism in their stance before life, and of helplessness in the way in which they set out some grim new report on the facts about human existence. No doubt it could be said that this was merely a transitional stage on the way to a freer, more open, less compromised

life structure; only when all the monsters have been stared down can men and women begin to live in the light. It can also be stated, as Breton said in 1945, that Surrealism was specifically an interwar movement: a miming, between one world war and another, of tensions which we should otherwise have been happy to overlook. The early warning system had implications which went far beyond private life; and it is certainly true that many of the masterpieces of Surrealism make perfect sense when read in this way. Giacometti's *Woman with Her Throat Cut* of 1932 (fig. 35) becomes a portrait of Europe, laid flat on her back and summarily done to death. Max Ernst's *The Horde* of 1927 (fig. 37) becomes even more explicit in the light of Hitler's coming to power in 1933. Miró's *Head of a Woman* of 1938 (pl. IX) has an aggres-

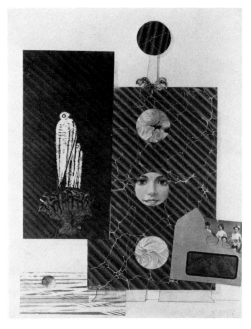

34. Max Ernst
The Postman Cheval, 1929–30
Peggy Guggenheim Foundation, Venice

35. Alberto Giacometti
Woman with Her Throat Cut, 1932 (cast 1949)
The Museum of Modern Art, New York

In the heyday of Surrealism the picture postcard was treasured by poets and painters alike for its direct and unsophisticated expression of popular feeling. At the end of the 1920s Max Ernst began to introduce postcards into collages both as themselves and as formal elements in a design whose intention was to please, to amuse, and sometimes to dismay. *The Postman Cheval* is named after a postman who had lately come to notice for the major contribution which he had made, spontaneously and without pretension, to naive or self-taught art; and, sure enough, the postcard in the lower right-hand corner comes in an envelope such as Cheval the postman must have carried every day on his rounds. But the point of the picture lies also in the contrast between the pretty but undeniably fallen women on the postcard and the conventional attributes of youth and innocence which abound elsewhere. Apart from the variations of space and texture which further thicken the plot, Ernst has penciled in beneath the largest rectangular form in the picture a pair of stylized feet which suggest that somewhere behind the main image is a sandwichboard-man for whom the day's task has been altogether too much.

sivity which would verge on dementia if we did not associate it with the civil war which had broken out in Miró's own country. Nobody would call Dali a profound political thinker, but his *Soft Construction with Boiled Beans: Premonition of Civil War,* 1936 (pl. X), gives us an unforgettable image of how society can tear itself apart in a specific landscape and under a specific sun.

There would be no difficulty, therefore, in presenting Surrealism in terms of premonitory illustration. A panorama like Max Ernst's *Europe After the Rain,* 1940–42 (fig. 36), offers few problems in that context, since history caught up with it almost before the paint was dry. There is a distinction, of course, between someone like Ernst, who lived in his own person the dramas of Europe between 1918 and 1945, or like Joan Miró, who even in his late 70s was willing to undergo real physical discomfort in order to demonstrate against social injustice, and those whose activity was primarily parasitic: parasitic on the horrors of war, and parasitic on the psychiatric case histories which still made novel reading in the 1920s and '30s. Miró and Ernst were not "history painters" in the conventional sense; but they functioned as irreplaceable witnesses to a crucial moment in European history.

X. Salvador Dali
Soft Construction with Boiled Beans:
    Premonition of Civil War, 1936
Philadelphia Museum of Art

Dali gave this painting its auxiliary title just six months before civil war broke out in his native Spain. In a picture which transcends the private and the particular, he sets before us an unforgettable image of a people tormented beyond endurance.

XI. Joan Miró
Object, 1936
The Museum of Modern Art, New York

At first glance this *Object* may seem purely nonsensical. But in point of fact everything in it relates to a logical sequence of associations. The hat stands for the archetypal dreamer, the red plastic fish for the uncharted deeps which are the domain of the unconscious, and the map for the universe through which the mind ranges freely. The heightened sexuality which is fundamental to Surrealism is symbolized by the gartered female leg in its high-heeled shoe. The parrot is, in this context, the bird of love. The ball which hangs from a piece of string is, once again, a familiar Surrealist symbol; pioneered by Giacometti in a sculpture well known to Miró, it stands for masculinity.

   Object is therefore a poem about love: soon un-riddled once we know how to read Miró's work.

36. Max Ernst
Europe After the Rain II, 1940–42
Wadsworth Atheneum, Hartford, Conn.

One of the most prescient and dismaying of 20th-century images is *Europe After the Rain,* which Max Ernst began in France, smuggled out of Europe, and completed in the United States. It has to do with a Europe overwhelmed by catastrophe, in which all distinctions between animal, vegetable and mineral are abolished and a universal desolation reigns.

37. Max Ernst
The Horde, 1927
Stedelijk Museum, Amsterdam

The European imagination has always been sensitive—and with good reason— to the notion of an invading army which would carry all before it. Through the centuries Tartars, Mongols and Turks took it in turn to personify that ravening horde; but by 1927, when Max Ernst painted *The Horde,* psychology had put forward the idea of the horde that is within each one of us and will destroy us if we do not hold it in check.

Yet the final, decisive, irreversible claim of the major Surrealists upon us does not derive from their stature as poetical commentators on a Europe far gone toward self-destruction. Nor does it derive from their skill at mapping the interior landscapes which had previously been kept hidden from sight: the glassy, detailed and hypnotic arenas to which Dali and Tanguy, above all, had access. What puts them in the Pantheon is the scale of their contribution to something quite different: the science of signs.

THE SCIENCE OF SIGNS

By "the science of signs" I mean the wordless communication system by which we agree to receive messages from one another. The science of signs is about the things in that system which can be taken for granted. The hunter goes along with it when he puts on the red shirt which saves him from getting shot. The pirate went along with it when he hoisted the black flag at sea. Hospitals count on it when they paint a red cross on their roofs in time of war. Such things are pure convention, but they work because we want them to work.

Art is the most highly evolved manifestation of the science of signs. Were it to stagnate in that respect it would forfeit its claim upon us; and it is because the Surrealists did not allow it to stagnate in the 1920s and early '30s that people today go along with visual acrobatics that would have been way beyond their capacity 50 years ago. Surrealism taught us, for instance, that the step-by-step narrative systems of the 19th century were not the only ones. It taught us that surprise may be the beginnings of wisdom. It taught us to deal simultaneously with pieces of information that zero in on us at differing levels and in differing guises. It taught us that what "doesn't make sense" may sometimes make the best sense of all. It taught us to watch out in everyday life for the poetic and mysterious connections for which one or two men of genius had noted the prototypes. It taught us, finally, that there is no pattern of life so pedestrian that it cannot be transformed by poetic principle, nor any combination of objects so pointless that a valid connection cannot be made between them. (Picasso made this last point once and for all when he made a most lifelike head of a bull from the saddle and the handlebars of a bicycle.)

Surrealism has long ago broken out of those areas of human activity which we label "art" and "literature." It is present in design, in film, in advertising, in humor, in dress—in the form of a general acceptance of incongruities which would once have been dismissed as meaningless nonsense. Sometimes one and the same man is still doing it: Luis Buñuel, for one, whose movies of the 1970s have fundamentally the same allegiances as they had in 1930, when Max Ernst played a bit part for him in *L'Age d'or*. But most often Surrealism has simply passed into the bloodstream of modern life like a benign virus, leaving the collective imagination by just that much the more liberated. Its ciphers have been cracked, and it is by now an instrument in everyday use; it does not, for instance, occur to the stand-up comic to call himself a Surrealist when he uses the quick cut and the one-line gag in ways perfected by Surrealist writers in the 1920s, any more than the automobile manufacturer claims the title when someone points out to him that his new season's models are being pub-

38. Joan Miró
Dutch Interior I, 1928
The Museum of Modern Art, New York

In 1928–29 Miró made a number of free adaptations of 16th- and 17th-century paintings of a relatively conventional sort. The given facts were metamorphosed, first in pencil in a small notebook which Miró carried in his pocket, later in full-scale paintings such as this one. The point of departure was H. M. Sorgh's *The Lutanist*, which Miró had seen in the Rijksmuseum in Amsterdam. But the original image was added to, subtracted from, readjusted in scale, and generally subjected to an imaginative reconstruction of a most thoroughgoing sort.

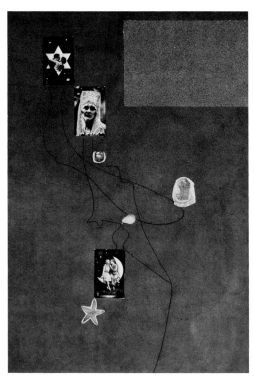

39. Max Ernst
*Loplop Introduces Members of the Surrealist
  Group,* 1931
The Museum of Modern Art, New York

As in *All Friends Together* (fig. 15) Max Ernst
in this collage assembles some active members of
the Surrealist group: among them Tristan Tzara,
Paul Eluard, Salvador Dali, Alberto Giacometti,
Man Ray, Yves Tanguy and Ernst himself. (New-
comers since 1922 also include the film director
Luis Buñuel.) The general environment is,
however, distinctly more somber: the masked
figure at the top could be an executioner, and at
the bottom on the left André Breton, self-
appointed dictator of the group, is seen swim-
ming—perhaps for his life—beside what might
well be a sinking ship.

40. Joan Miró
Rope and People I, 1935
The Museum of Modern Art, New York

The mid-1930s were a time of anguish for all thinking
Europeans. Miró got something of this into *Rope
and People* by implying that the man on the left was
not just "biting his nails" in anxiety, but on the edge
of biting his whole hand off. Miró confirmed many
years later that he imagined the twisted skein of
rope as "binding and torturing" the three human
beings in the picture: and he carried over into the
two women on the right the sensations of helpless
disarray with which people waited for the worst and
knew that it could not be long delayed.

41. Joan Miró
Drawing-Collage, 1933
The Museum of Modern Art, New York

Joan Miró and Max Ernst were first associated in
1926, when they collaborated on a ballet for
Diaghilev: *Romeo and Juliet.* In the summer of
1933 Miró amused himself with a series of
"drawing-collages" which can be related to comparable works (fig. 39) by Max Ernst. This particular
one has a covert mathematical basis in the
relation of the postcards to the collaged piece of
sandpaper, and of the sandpaper in its turn to
the format of the work as a whole. The three
postcards are used half in mischief and half in
wonder, as indications of popular feeling. Miró
then comments on their idealized account of
sexuality by adding four quite different images,
each of which has a more down-to-earth implication. Finally, he linked these disparate images
with a freehand drawing that touches discreetly
on the facts of the female body and on the
potential of its involvement with the male.

42. Henry Moore
Reclining Figure, 1937
Fogg Art Museum, Harvard University, Cambridge, Mass.

43. Jean (Hans) Arp
Human Concretion, 1935
The Museum of Modern Art, New York

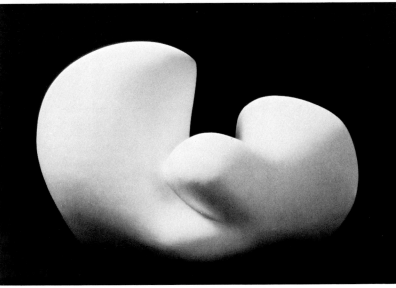

Surrealism was very strong on forms that echo the human figure but do not represent it. Sometimes, as in Arp's *Human Concretion,* the human body seemed to curl in upon itself. At other times, as in the tough-minded, shoelike *Reclining Figure* of Henry Moore, the body and its natural ridges and protuberances were completely reinvented and left to fend for themselves as objects independent of Nature.

44. Alberto Giacometti
No More Play, 1933
Julien Levy, Bridgewater, Conn.

Among symbolical objects in everyday use the game board (chess, checkers, backgammon) stands high. Giacometti in 1933 invented a game board of his own: a mysterious terrain, a matter of deep hollows and coffinlike indentations on which the door could be shut fast. In the midst of this were human figures that were left stranded at the end of the game, with nowhere to go.

licized in ways lifted straight from the paintings of Magritte.

The initial statements retain their magic, even so. The moment at which something new was added to the science of signs is as significant as ever it was. The additions are of many kinds, but dreams and the dreamer are somewhere at the back of most of them. In 1929, for instance, a long series of poetical objects by Giacometti was prefaced by his *Reclining Woman Who Dreams.* In that series, Giacometti never repeated himself. Each idea was used once and for all, and the function of the dream was to let fresh air into the problem, "How can sculpture continue?" From 1925 to 1933 he probed and reprobed the poetics of art to see just what kind of magic could be made with objects that were unlike anything that had borne the name of art before. Sometimes they came in cages, in ways that were taken up in later years by artists of quite other persuasions. Sometimes they were like freakish kitchen utensils; sometimes, like scale models of the terrain on which some new kind of ball game would one day be played. He made no claims for them—to the point of naming some of them as "disagreeable objects of no value which should be thrown away." But they turned out, all the same, to enlarge the science of signs.

"Surrealist" is too narrow a word for the best of what has been

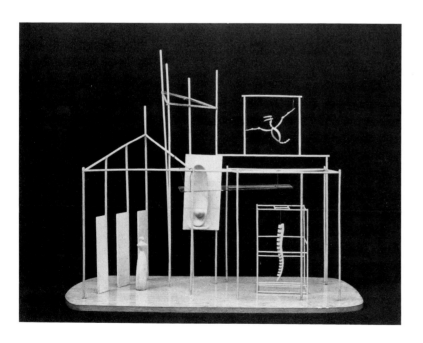

45. Alberto Giacometti
The Palace at 4 A.M., 1932–33
The Museum of Modern Art, New York

In the summer of 1932 Giacometti built and rebuilt, every night, a palace of matchsticks. From this there came in time one of the most haunting and influential of modern sculptures: *The Palace at 4 A.M.* It is haunting for its uncanny mingling of practicality and the dream. It has been influential because it exemplifies the idea that sculpture can be open, skeletal, and all but incorporeal, rather than solid, weighty, and self-consciously monumental. The roofless and wall-less palace is open to inspection from every angle. The spinal column in the cage on the right stands for the woman with whom the nights in question were spent. The figure on the left in a floor-length skirt represents Giacometti's mother, "just as she appears," he wrote, "in my earliest memories." The thrice-repeated curtain on the left is "the very curtain I saw when I opened my eyes for the first time." The skeleton bird (above right) stands for the birds which signaled the approach of a new day at 4 A.M. that summer, and in particular "the very night before the morning in which our life together collapsed." As for the object halfway up the broken tower in the middle, we remember that in 1926 Giacometti made a sculpture called *Spoon Woman*; and here, six years later, is a spoon man, the sculptor himself, close to and yet apart from the two women who meant most to him.

46. René Magritte
Private Diary 1, 1951
Mr. and Mrs. Max Wasserman, Chestnut Hill, Mass.

To get a piece of grit in one's eye is one of the more painful of everyday misadventures. But what if we were *all* grit? Men of stone, for whom the mishap could have no meaning? Magritte reverses the conditions of life—and by doing so causes us to think new thoughts about them.

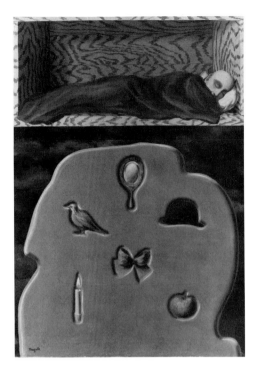

47. René Magritte
The Reckless Sleeper, 1927
The Tate Gallery, London

The cannon as instrument of aggression and the cannon as phallic symbol had been familiar in Surrealist painting since the early days of de Chirico (fig. 9). It presides, here, over an anthology of Magritte's favorite subjects—among them the straight-faced townhouses of suburban Brussels, the bells that pick up the slightest breeze, the detail of a particularly handsome female torso, and the forest through which Magritte's horsemen will shortly come at a canter.

48. René Magritte
On the Threshold of Liberty, 1929
Museum Boymans-van Beuningen, Rotterdam

XII. René Magritte
The Pleasant Truth, 1966
Private collection, U.S.A.

Magritte projects onto a characteristically massive and heavily shadowed section of wall an image based on the traditional iconography of the Last Supper. Its phantomatic quality is emphasized by the fact that the superimposed image sometimes comes forward (as in the turretlike folds of the cloth) and sometimes retreats backward (as with the food on the table).

42

49. René Magritte
The Domain of Arnheim, 1962
Madame René Magritte, Brussels

The title comes from Edgar Allan Poe. The image is pure Magritte, and it suggests a changed world in which the eagle in its eyrie is one with the mountain top.

How did the eggs get there? Did the eagle turn back to flesh, blood and feathers? Magritte isn't telling, but the problems add a further turn of the screw to what is as haunting a "Tale of the Grotesque" as any of the ones which made Poe's reputation.

50. René Magritte
Euclid's Walks, 1955
The Minneapolis Institute of Arts

cepted by the Parisian Surrealists, who thought of him, alike in his work and in his habits of life, as altogether too prosaic. And it is true that we never get from Magritte what we get from a Miró of the late 1920s—the sense of the painting as an arena in which literally any combination of signs can be accepted as valid. Magritte had certain specifically Belgian traits, and his procedures were slow-moving, workmanlike, and unfailingly regular in the beat of their pulse. The unconscious did not present itself to him as a dancing dervish. Yet when it came to restating the science of signs no one was more radical than he.

He did it under auspices with which the reader will by now be familiar. Nowhere is the dreamer more vividly portrayed or more bizarrely accompanied. The spirit of Edgar Allan Poe hovers over and over again, with *The Narrative of Arthur Gordon Pym* conspicuous in one painting and the whole of another one devoted to Poe's *Domain of Arnheim*. Magritte realized, too, that the mass audience thriller (see his *The Menaced Assassin*, pl. III) was one of our century's new sources of myth. He had a delight in word games which had been the mark of the Surrealists since long before the name of Surrealism was first invented; and he knew that when language is subverted the whole of life is subverted with it. He was interested in the word *as sign*—and as a sign that should not be taken for granted. When he wrote "This is not a pipe" beneath a painted image of a pipe, people took it at first as a harmless little joke; but as time went on it turned out that the joke was not so harmless after all, and that Magritte had questioned the whole nature of acceptance where the science of signs was concerned. "Go back and start again" is the message which he relays to those who look at his pictures; and by looking again, and looking again, and looking more closely, we arrive at a new understanding of the role of the sign in human life. Magritte, in this sense, can be related to linguistic philosophy as other Surrealists can be related to the psychopathology of the individual, or to the state of the European collective unconscious at a particular moment in time, or to the liberation of the play instinct in everyday life, or to one of the many other preoccupations of the 1920s and '30s which found their highest and most telling expression in art. Looking back on the two decades in question, we may well be reminded of what the British scientist J. Z. Young wrote in his *Introduction to the Study of Man* (1971): "There is a case for saying that the creation of new aesthetic forms has been the most fundamentally productive of all forms of human activity. Whoever creates new artistic conventions has found methods of interchange between people about matters which were incommunicable before. The capacity to do this has been the basis of the whole of human history."

discussed here. It resulted, that is to say, from Surrealism and *from something else:* from a thoughtful scrutiny of Cubism, in Giacometti's case; from an interaction with the distant past of German art in the case of Max Ernst; from an atavistic tradition of Roman *gravitas* in the case of Giorgio de Chirico. Surrealism in such instances was the leaven, or the well-timed explosive, or even at times the latecomer who tidied things up and demanded all the credit. "If it's good, annex it" was the order of the day among the official Surrealists.

A case in point is that of the Belgian painter René Magritte. Magritte at one time lived in Paris, but he was never quite ac-

SUGGESTED READINGS

Surrealism

Alexandrian, Sarane. *Surrealist World.* (World of Art ser.)
New York, Praeger, 1970.

Balakian, Anna. *Surrealism: The Road to the Absolute.* Rev. ed.
New York, E. P. Dutton, 1970.

Barr, Alfred H., Jr. *Fantastic Art, Dada, Surrealism.* Reprint. First publ. 1937.
New York, Arno for The Museum of Modern Art, 1970.

Bigsby, C. W. *Dada and Surrealism.* (The Critical Idiom ser.)
London, Methuen; New York, Barnes and Noble, 1972.

Breton, André. *Manifestoes of Surrealism.* Seaver, Richard, and Lane, Helen, tr.
Ann Arbor, University of Michigan Press, 1972.

Breton, André. *Surrealism and Painting.* Watson Taylor, Simon, tr.
(Icon Editions ser.)
New York, Harper and Row, 1972.

Janis, Sidney. *Abstract and Surrealist Art in America.* (Contemporary Art ser.)
Reprint. First publ. 1944. New York, Arno, 1970.

Levy, Julien. *Surrealism.* Reprint. First publ. 1936.
(Co-publ. by Worldwide Reprints.) New York, Arno, 1968.

Lippard, Lucy, ed. *Surrealists on Art.*
Englewood Cliffs, N.J., Prentice-Hall, 1970.

Morris, C. B. *Surrealism and Spain.*
New York, Cambridge University Press, 1972.

Ray, Paul. *Surrealist Movement in England.*
Ithaca, N.Y., Cornell University Press, 1971.

Read, Herbert. *Surrealism.*
New York, Praeger, 1972.

Rubin, William. *Dada and Surrealist Art.*
New York, Abrams, 1969.

Rubin, William. *Dada, Surrealism, and Their Heritage.*
New York, The Museum of Modern Art, 1968.

Sandrow, Nahura. *Surrealism: Theater, Art, Ideas.*
New York, Harper and Row, 1972.

Waldberg, Patrick. *Surrealism.*
New York, McGraw-Hill, 1966.

Jean (Hans) Arp

Arp, Jean. *On My Way: Poetry and Essays 1912–1947.*
New York, Wittenborn, Schultz, 1948.

Jean, Marcel, ed. *Arp on Arp.* (Documents of 20th-Century Art ser.)
New York, Viking, 1972.

Read, Herbert. *The Art of Jean Arp.*
New York, Abrams, 1968.

Soby, James Thrall. *Arp.*
New York, The Museum of Modern Art, 1958.

Trier, Eduard. *Jean Arp: Sculpture. His Last Ten Years.*
New York, Abrams, 1968.

Giorgio de Chirico

Carrà, Massimo. *Metaphysical Art.*
Rathke, Ewald; Waldberg, Patrick; and Tisdall, Caroline, eds.
New York, Praeger, 1972.

Chirico, Giorgio de. *The Memoirs of Giorgio de Chirico.*
Crosland, Margaret, tr.
Coral Gables, Fla., University of Miami Press, 1971.

Far, Isabella. *Giorgio de Chirico.*
New York, Abrams, 1969.

Soby, James Thrall. *Giorgio de Chirico.* Reprint. First publ. 1955.
New York, Arno for The Museum of Modern Art, 1966.

Salvador Dali

Bosquet, Alain. *Conversations with Dali.*
New York, E. P. Dutton, 1969.

Dali, Salvador. *Dali by Dali.*
New York, Abrams, 1972.

Lake, Carlton. *In Quest of Dali.*
New York, Putnam, 1969.

Max, Gerard. *Dali.*
New York, Abrams, 1968.

Soby, James Thrall. *Salvador Dali.* Reprint. First publ. 1946.
New York, Arno for The Museum of Modern Art, 1970.

Max Ernst

Alexandrian, Sarane. *Max Ernst.*
Chicago and Los Angeles, O'Hara, 1972.

Chevalier, Denys. *Max Ernst.*
New York, Crown, 1972.

Ernst, Max. *Beyond Painting and Other Writings by the Artist and His Friends.*
(Documents of Modern Art ser.)
New York, Wittenborn, 1948.

Lieberman, William S. *Max Ernst*. Reprint. First publ. 1961.
New York, Arno for The Museum of Modern Art, 1972.

Russell, John. *Max Ernst: Life and Work*.
New York, Abrams, 1967.

Schneede, Uwe M. *The Essential Max Ernst*.
London, Thames and Hudson, 1972.

Spies, Werner. *The Return of La Belle Jardinière. Max Ernst 1950–1970*.
New York, Abrams, 1971.

Alberto Giacometti

Lust, Herbert. *Giacometti: The Complete Graphics*.
New York, Tudor, 1970.

Hohl, Reinhold. *Alberto Giacometti*.
New York, Abrams, 1972.

René Magritte

Gablik, Suzi. *Magritte*.
Greenwich, Conn., New York Graphic Society, 1970.

Passeron, René. *René Magritte*.
Chicago and Los Angeles, O'Hara, 1972.

Soby, James Thrall. *René Magritte*.
New York, The Museum of Modern Art, 1966.

Sylvester, David. *René Magritte*.
New York, Praeger, 1969.

Waldberg, Patrick. *René Magritte*.
New York, Wittenborn, 1965.

André Masson

Brownstone, Gilbert. *Masson*.
New York, Wittenborn, 1970.

Hahn, Otto. *Masson*. (Modern Artists ser.)
New York, Abrams, 1965.

Joan Miró

Bonnefoy, Yves. *Miró*.
London, Studio Vista; New York, Viking, 1967.

Dupin, Jacques. *Miró Sculpture*.
New York, Macmillan, 1972.

Greenberg, Clement. *Joan Miró*. (Contemporary Art ser.)
Reprint. First publ. 1948. New York, Arno, 1970.

Penrose, Roland. *Miró*.
New York, Abrams, 1969.

Rubin, William. *Miró in the Collection of The Museum of Modern Art*.
New York, The Museum of Modern Art, 1973.

Soby, James Thrall. *Joan Miró*.
New York, The Museum of Modern Art, 1959.

Sweeney, James J. *Joan Miró*. Reprint. First publ. 1941.
New York, Arno for The Museum of Modern Art, 1970.

Taillandier, Yvon. *The Indelible Miró*.
New York, Tudor, 1972.

Tapié, Michel. *Joan Miró*.
New York, Abrams, 1970.

LIST OF ILLUSTRATIONS

Dimensions: height precedes width; another dimension, depth, is given for sculptures and constructions where relevant. Foreign titles are in English, except in cases where the title does not translate or is better known in its original form. Asterisked titles indicate works reproduced in color.

Arp, Jean (Hans)
(1887–1966)

Human Concretion, 1935 (fig. 43)
Original plaster, 19½ x 18¾ inches
The Museum of Modern Art, New York
Gift of the Advisory Committee

Balthus (Baltusz Klossowski de Rola)
(b. 1908)

The Mountain, 1937 (fig. 3)
Oil on canvas, 8 feet 2 inches x 11 feet 11 inches
Private collection, New York

Bellmer, Hans
(b. 1902)

Machinegun (La Mitrailleuse), 1937 (fig. 26)
(restored by the artist 1965)
Wood, metal and papier-mâché,
30⅞ x 29¾ x 13⅝ inches
The Museum of Modern Art, New York
Purchase

Carrà, Carlo
(1881–1966)

Metaphysical Muse, 1917 (fig. 11)
Oil on canvas, 36 x 26¼ inches
Emilio Jesi, Milan

Cézanne, Paul
(1839–1906)

The Murder, c. 1870 (fig. 2)
Oil on canvas, 25½ x 32¼ inches
The Walker Art Gallery, Liverpool

Chirico, Giorgio de
(b. 1888)

*The Anxious Journey, 1913 (pl. I)
Oil on canvas, 29¼ x 42 inches
The Museum of Modern Art, New York
Acquired through the Lillie P. Bliss Bequest

Song of Love, 1914 (fig. 6)
Oil on canvas, 28¾ x 23½ inches
Private collection, New York

The Philosopher's Conquest, 1914 (fig. 9)
Oil on canvas, 49½ x 39¼ inches
The Art Institute of Chicago
The Joseph Winterbotham Collection

The Child's Brain, 1914 (fig. 8)
Oil on canvas, 32 x 26 inches
Nationalmuseum, Stockholm

The Mystery and Melancholy of a Street, 1914
(fig. 13)
Oil on canvas, 34¼ x 28⅛ inches
Mr. and Mrs. Stanley S. Resor, New Canaan, Conn.

The Evil Genius of a King, 1914–15 (fig. 7)
Oil on canvas, 24 x 19¾ inches
The Museum of Modern Art, New York
Purchase

The Mathematicians, 1917 (fig. 10)
Pencil, 12¾ x 8⅝ inches
The Museum of Modern Art, New York
Gift of Mrs. Stanley Resor

Dali, Salvador
(b. 1904)

Illumined Pleasures, 1929 (fig. 28)
Oil and collage on composition board,
9⅜ x 13¾ inches
The Museum of Modern Art, New York
The Sidney and Harriet Janis Collection

The Persistence of Memory, 1931 (fig. 29)
Oil on canvas, 9½ x 13 inches
The Museum of Modern Art, New York
Given anonymously

The Birth of Liquid Desires, 1932 (fig. 27)
Oil on canvas, 37⅜ x 44⅛ inches
Peggy Guggenheim Foundation, Venice

*Soft Construction with Boiled Beans: Premonition
of Civil War, 1936 (pl. X)
Oil on canvas, 39⅜ x 39 inches
Philadelphia Museum of Art
The Louise and Walter Arensberg Collection

Elmer, Edwin Romanzo
(1850–1923)

Mourning Picture, c. 1889 (fig. 5)
Oil on canvas, 28 x 36 inches
Smith College Museum of Art, Northampton,
Mass.

Ernst, Max
(b. 1891)

The Little Tear Gland That Says Tic Tac, 1920
(fig. 14)
Wallpaper borders altered with gouache,
14¼ x 10 inches
The Museum of Modern Art, New York
Purchase

All Friends Together, 1922 (fig. 15)
Oil on canvas, 52 x 78 inches
Wallraf-Richartz-Museum, Cologne

*Pietà or Revolution by Night, 1923 (pl. II)
Oil on canvas, 46¼ x 35½ inches
Private collection, Turin

*Two Children Are Threatened by a Nightingale,
1924 (pl. VI)
Oil on wood with wood construction,
27½ x 22½ x 4½ inches
The Museum of Modern Art, New York
Purchase

Sheet from Histoire Naturelle, 1926 (fig. 24)
Portfolio of collotypes, after frottages, 19⅝ x 12½
inches
The Museum of Modern Art, New York
Gift of James Thrall Soby

The Big Forest, 1927 (fig. 32)
Oil on canvas, 45½ x 58¼ inches
Kunstmuseum, Basel

The Horde, 1927 (fig. 37)
Oil on canvas, 44⅞ x 57½ inches
Stedelijk Museum, Amsterdam

The Postman Cheval, 1929–30 (fig. 34)
Collage on pasteboard, 25¼ x 18⅞ inches
Peggy Guggenheim Foundation, Venice

Loplop Introduces Members of the Surrealist
Group, 1931 (fig. 39)
Pasted photographs and pencil, 19¾ x 13¼
inches
The Museum of Modern Art, New York
Purchase

Three pages from Une Semaine de bonté (fig. 25)
(a book of engravings in 5 volumes)
Editions Jeanne Bucher, Paris, 1934

*The Angel of Hearth and Home, 1937 (pl. VII)
Oil on canvas, 45½ x 58¼ inches
Private collection, Paris

Europe After the Rain II, 1940–42 (fig. 36)
Oil on canvas, 21½ x 58¾ inches
Wadsworth Atheneum, Hartford, Conn.

Fuseli, Henry
(1741–1825)

The Nightmare, 1781 (fig. 1)
Oil on canvas, 40 x 50 inches
The Detroit Institute of Arts
Gift of Mr. and Mrs. Bert L. Smokler and
Mr. and Mrs. Lawrence A. Fleischman

Giacometti, Alberto
(1901–1966)

Woman with Her Throat Cut, 1932 (fig. 35)
Bronze (cast 1949), 34½ x 25 inches
The Museum of Modern Art, New York
Purchase

The Palace at 4 A.M., 1932–33 (fig. 45)
Construction in wood, glass, wire and string,
25 x 28¼ x 15¾ inches
The Museum of Modern Art, New York
Purchase

No More Play, 1933 (fig. 44)
Marble, wood and bronze, 23 x 17⅝ inches
Julien Levy, Bridgewater, Conn.

Grosz, George
(1893–1959)

Republican Automatons, 1920 (fig. 12)
Watercolor, 23⅝ x 18⅝ inches
The Museum of Modern Art, New York
Advisory Committee Fund

Klinger, Max
(1857–1920)

The Glove, No. 7: "The Nightmare," 1878–80
(fig. 4) from a series of 10 etchings,
published by the artist, Berlin, 1881 (Opus VI)
Etching, 5⅝ x 10⅝ inches (plate)
The Museum of Modern Art, New York
Purchase

Magritte, René
(1898–1967)

*The Menaced Assassin, 1926 (pl. III)
Oil on canvas, 59¼ x 77 inches
The Museum of Modern Art, New York
Kay Sage Tanguy Fund

The Reckless Sleeper, 1927 (fig. 47)
Oil on canvas, 45¼ x 31¼ inches
The Tate Gallery, London

On the Threshold of Liberty, 1929 (fig. 48)
Oil on canvas, 45⅜ x 57⅞ inches
Museum Boymans-van Beuningen, Rotterdam

Private Diary 1, 1951 (fig. 46)
Oil on canvas, 25½ x 31½ inches
Mr. and Mrs. Max Wasserman, Chestnut Hill,
    Mass.

Euclid's Walks, 1955 (fig. 50)
Oil on canvas, 64⅛ x 51⅛ inches
The Minneapolis Institute of Arts
The William Hood Dunwoody Fund

The Domain of Arnheim, 1962 (fig. 49)
Oil on canvas, 57⅝ x 44⅞ inches
Madame René Magritte, Brussels

*The Pleasant Truth, 1966 (pl. XII)
Oil on canvas, 35⅛ x 51⅛ inches
Private collection, U.S.A.

Masson, André
(b. 1896)

*Painting (Figure), 1927 (pl. V)
Oil and sand on canvas, 18 x 10½ inches
The Museum of Modern Art, New York
Gift of William Rubin

Miró, Joan
(b. 1893)

Portrait of E. C. Ricart (called The Man in Pyjamas),
    1917 (fig. 17)
Oil and print glued on canvas, 31⅞ x 25⅝ inches
The Museum of Modern Art, New York
Extended loan of the Florene May
    Schoenborn and Samuel A. Marx Collection

View of Montroig, 1917 (fig. 16)
Oil on canvas, 26⅛ x 29 inches
The Solomon R. Guggenheim Museum, New York

Portrait of a Woman, 1918 (fig. 18)
Oil on canvas, 27½ x 24½ inches
The Art Institute of Chicago
The Joseph Winterbotham Collection

The Table (Still Life with Rabbit), 1920 (fig. 20)
Oil on canvas, 52 x 44 inches
Gustav Zumsteg, Zürich

Table with Glove, 1921 (fig. 19)
Oil on canvas, 46 x 35¼ inches
The Museum of Modern Art, New York
Gift of Armand G. Erpf

The Hunter (Catalan Landscape), 1923–24 (fig. 23)
Oil on canvas, 25½ x 39½ inches
The Museum of Modern Art, New York
Purchase

The Tilled Field, 1923–24 (fig. 21)
Oil on canvas, 26 x 37 inches
The Solomon R. Guggenheim Museum, New York

Carnival of Harlequin, 1924–25 (fig. 22)
Oil on canvas, 26 x 36⅝ inches
Albright-Knox Art Gallery, Buffalo, N.Y.

*The Birth of the World, 1925 (pl. IV)
Oil on canvas, 98¾ x 78¾ inches
The Museum of Modern Art, New York
Purchase

Dutch Interior I, 1928 (fig. 38)
Oil on canvas, 36⅛ x 28¾ inches
The Museum of Modern Art, New York
Mrs. Simon Guggenheim Fund

Drawing-Collage, 1933 (fig. 41)
Collage and charcoal drawing on green paper
    with three postcards, sandpaper and four
    engravings, 42½ x 28⅜ inches
The Museum of Modern Art, New York
Kay Sage Tanguy Bequest

Rope and People I, 1935 (fig. 40)
Oil on cardboard with coil of rope, 41¼ x 29⅜
    inches
The Museum of Modern Art, New York
Given anonymously

*Object, 1936 (pl. XI)
Construction of hollowed wooden post, stuffed
    parrot on wooden stand, hat, and map,
    31⅞ x 11⅞ x 10¼ inches
The Museum of Modern Art, New York
Gift of Mr. and Mrs. Pierre Matisse

*Head of a Woman, 1938 (pl. IX)
Oil on canvas, 22 x 18¼ inches
The Minneapolis Institute of Arts

Moore, Henry
(b: 1898)

Reclining Figure, 1937 (fig. 42)
Hopton-wood stone, 33 inches long
Fogg Art Museum, Harvard University,
    Cambridge, Mass

Oppenheim, Meret
(b. 1913)

Object, 1936 (fig. 33)
Fur-covered teacup, saucer and spoon,
    2⅞ inches high
The Museum of Modern Art, New York
Purchase

Picasso, Pablo
(1881–1973)

Seated Bather, 1930 (fig. 30)
Oil on canvas, 64¼ x 51 inches
The Museum of Modern Art, New York
Mrs. Simon Guggenheim Fund

Model and Surrealist Figure, 1933 (fig. 31)
Etching
Page from Picasso for Vollard, published
    by Harry N. Abrams, New York, 1956.

Tanguy, Yves
(1900–1955)

*Mama, Papa Is Wounded! 1927 (pl. VIII)
Oil on canvas, 36¼ inches x 28¾ inches
The Museum of Modern Art, New York
Purchase